A LITTLE LITTLE TALK

BY

MICHELLE JEAN

God we can no longer live by the rules of sin anymore
Humanity cannot fear for their lives anymore
The lies have gone on for far too long and something must be done immediately

God I will ask again where is the regard for life?
Where are you in all of this?

You cannot keep closed mouth because death cannot control you nor can death touch you

God come on now. Sin steals our identity and death takes from you but all that death takes does not belong to death. Sure all of humanity belongs to death but the trees and air, the water we drink does not belong to death it belongs to you.

Oh I forgot man have given the air, the trees and waters over to death and I need not mention the fire because the fire always belonged to sin and death. So yes I stand corrected. Better yet God forget this thought because it will lead to nowhere apart from hell.

Michelle

Okay God because I want to know the truth

Why doesn't death torment you? Come on now God why doesn't death torment you why does death have to torment me? Yes I know death can't touch you nor can death come near you because where you reside is pure and clean but why me? Why does sin and death come knocking at my door? For a change why doesn't death reach out to you? Yes I know better but for a change I want to see sin and death try. Lovey you know the reason why. Today I am being mischievous because I know better. Well I know sin and death is scared of you and neither one have the balls to confront you. Lovey this I know plus I know sin and death knows not the pathway onto you so they cannot come close nor can they torment you.

Okay God forget this one too because I know the answers to my questions and I should not terrorize you in this way because I know better but God truly why does sin and death have to terrorize man – humanity.

Oh man I am becoming sad but Lovey oblige me here because I sound worse than a broken record but God no one on the face of this planet can say sin and death is not true because every culture and race know sin and death is true. Sin can only be true to sin which is paid out in debt sorry death.

Lovey, truly look down upon us and see the damage we have done to a once beautiful and serene planet.

We caused you to flee to a cleaner home and that was not fear to you but what can I do because soon death will come knocking at my door but I ask of you do not let the same death angel take me. Meaning do not let the death angel that take the life of sinful and wicked people as well as sinful and wicked spirits including animals take me. God if I am clean please let me stay clean and good and do not let the sins of death touch me or take my life.

God I cannot come to you dirty I have to come to you clean so please let my goodness cleanse me as well as cleanse my family and my family includes my peeps true loved ones and friends. All the good ones and yes all my good family.

MICHELLE

God it's not hard to see the destruction of this world.
It's not hard to see the extinction of humanity.

Lovey all that we do to kill Mother Earth this planet humanity cannot see that they too are killing self

Lovey it's a painful and dark day. I guess I will know the time and hour of the extinction of man when I see the moon turn black then I will know the end is here – near and all humanity will die a painful death

I have yet to see a black moon but with all that's going on on earth I don't think this vision will be far off. The bloodshed I constantly see because death is constantly before me so I don't let this phase me. When I see the fighting breaking out I just know each outcome in foreign lands become more dreadful – vile.

Yes I've seen many moons more recently a small white moon with a red ring at the bottom around it and it was being pulled towards me. I can't remember if I was the one pulling it but I know it was being pulled towards me. Lovey to me the red signifies danger and I am pulling danger towards me but no this is not danger this is a warning. It's like the white lady that was dressed in white with a red belly band. She was there to warn me telling me I was travelling on the wrong track and I was to get back on. But Lovey the moon am I truly pulling danger towards me with all that I write and say. I know many will be offended by the truth have to be told and God I cannot stress the importance of the truth anymore because like I've said and told you humanity live for death for death and not life. So because we have given death our lives as well as the life of our planet we will die – all must come to an end.

God this is not your will but the will of man – humanity and what is to be must be because we did sign our birth certificates over to death hence we all have a death certificate and not a birth certificate.

Lovey no one can blame you because all you did to educate humanity they chose not to listen. They chose to follow death so unto death they must go.

As for me God prepare a place for me and my family not just my kids but for my peeps true loved ones and friends. God because of their goodness include them in our family because they did sacrifice for you and now we will all begin our new journey as your children your true and righteous ones – the chosen few.

MICHELLE

God today I am not defeated I just feel like giving up

God today I cannot see my purpose in life and to be honest I don't want to die in vain nor do I want to die for sinful and wicked people

God Lovey we have lost our way and we deserve to know the truth
We deserve the truth – the full truth without any lies

Lovey I don't know but please lift the hands of death from around me because I know the hands of spiritual and physical evil

God whatever spiritual evil is doing to me lift your shield and surround me with your good and righteous protection and let the evil deeds of spiritual wickedness and evil fall back on them – the spiritual wicked

God whatever evil the devil has commissioned for me let it fall back on the devil. God leave no stone unturned and let every evil force great and small, bond and free, high and low turn back on evil and let me be free to prosper a good way like you ordained it to be. God never let this pledge be broken by anyone not even me or you. This is our pledge to defeat all evil and bound them to the pits of hell like it is suppose to be. God this time around none can be free because death will have them and I know death will never ever set them free.

God Lovey do not look upon my thoughts as vengeance but look upon it as freedom from our people. Lovey in all honesty because you know I cannot lie to you but let evil get a taste of his own medicine come on now. Lovey I am trying my best not to walk in the way of sin so let sin stay where he or she belongs and stay away from me.

Hon. I want nothing to do with sin all my wants needs and desires I need from you God not sin. Come on now Lovey who needs sin and death not me. I know the works of sin and death and I'm to want and desire that please. Lovey you and I both know that sin commission death but death is stronger than sin. Sin has no power over death because death is the one to take sins life in the end.

Lovey Satan and his agents have no power over death but he Satan has power over sin. Satan is the one to commission sin/evil hence evil is a part of Will and also a part of the makeup of this universe.

God Lovey Satan have to bow down to death. Satan runs from death. He seeks to hide by trying to buy time but in all that he does he cannot buy time nor can he buy death.

24000 years hath evil – sin but once that 24000 years is over his wicked people will die. Must die because in all they did they never thought about life they only thought about death but death never thought about them and cannot think of them. All death can do is kill them – take their life. This is their end because they did chose death and death paid them in return because death can only pay in death it can never pay them in life.

MICHELLE

Lovey as I come to you hold me tonight and never let me go
Lovey this is one of those nights that I need you beside me. I need you to hold me and tell me that everything is going to be alright

God I know what I need from you but yet in some ways I don't know
God I know that you are with me as well as there for me but yet I feel lost because I am going this alone

God sometimes I wish I had someone there with me in the physical. I know I know you are there with me but this is one of those days where I want to touch you, hold you and tell you my troubles face to face

Lovey why do we have to be so far apart?
God and Lovey I hate the distance I truly hate it it's so not right

I know you can do something but the uncleanness of this planet, the uncleanness of my heart and body keeps us apart.

God where can we meet that's clean?
Where can we meet just to say hello and goodbye see you soon?

My heart aches for you and I can't live on memories – stories

God what right do you have to alienate me – keep me at bay

Lovey we are miles apart trillions of miles to be exact but with all that is said and done I need you, need you close to me – nearby

Lovey I cannot do this without you. You have to give your consent. Please don't deny me you and see you real soon.

MICHELLE

A sadness for a love – true love that you cannot see although at times you know he is truly there

Beyond the field of dreams I stand I see me but I do not see you
Worlds apart
A different universe
A different language
A different place and time

Beyond the fields of dreams I stand
Waiting
Waiting to see you
Just to hear your voice
Touch you

Time lapse
Hope fades
Memories gone
No direction home

Beyond the field of dreams I sand I see me but I do not see you
I see me waiting for you but you never came. You left me standing there all alone

Beyond the field of dreams I stand I see me but I do not see you because in reality you are truly not there.

MICHELLE

God I cannot face the mountain alone
I cannot face the pain
Everyone has abandoned me
No one there to truly help direct me
Help me with the task at hand

I guess not everyone is clean and none has been selected by you to truly help me so I have to go it alone and truly infinitely truly rely on you to direct me home – direct me on the right path

God the loneliness of one being alone gets to me at times but hey what can I do? I have to face it – bare it

Lovey do you get lonely when I am not there? I mean its summer time well not yet summer but still spring in full bloom but the weather is nice I cannot complain but I would not mind a little rain where I am. The grass is not green and you know how I love and cherish green everything.

Hon. I don't know but it's like I want to fly away just jet away to Paris, Scotland. I need to go to Scotland to write. I don't know why but I have to go there and stay awhile before my life expires – well sorry time expires here on earth.

I would love to go to Russia too and yes visit Kenya beautiful Kenya for the entire world to see.

Lovey we truly need to connect and do some vacationing somewhere soon.

MICHELLE

God nowhere is safe for humanity
Sea creatures are doomed
The second wave of death is here because now the seaways are polluted humanity have done it. The extinction of man – humanity will be soon

It's not long now God before the fishes of the sea become not edible because of the dragons radiation poisoning.

This dragon God I know is not China but their counterpart

God what were they thinking?

Did revelations not warn man – humanity? It did but then again humanity reads revelations wrong

God what is humanity going to do because soon they won't be able to swim in the waters of the sea nor will they be able to eat the fishes of the sea.

God this woe will devastate humanity because the seas are now being poisoned by the carelessness of man – humanity. There greed have reached far and it will be this greed that devours them – destroy all of humanity.

Lovey we create diseases designed them to kill man – nations. This we call the human depletion the depletion of the human species the human race. But with all that is said God these designers fail to remember that they too are going to die. They will not escape the judgment because they along with sin and death went against the code and laws of life.

Woe be unto their families future their future generations because the blood of the innocent is on their hands because their fathers, mothers, sisters, brothers, ancestors made it so. Their families blood will now be on their hands and head because of the sins of their fathers and sin pass from generation to generation. This is how the debt is incurred because each one every man forgets that the debts of sin cannot be repaid in life but in death and all must die who have committed grave sins.

Death awaits them all with a smile on his face and trust me death will thoroughly enjoy.

MICHELLE

God evil and man – humanity have no conscience because everyone kill – play the dominion game, the control game, the blame game and in all that they do they fail to realize that no man or woman – not one thing human or spirit can control life and death.

Both these factors life and death governs the universe. It is negative and positive energy the makeup of life – it is essential.

God you are the only one that can control these forces. You are All otherwise known to man as Allelujah. Good and evil must call on your name. God and Lovey you do not dominate or control because both meaning life and death have free Will and this is negative and positive energy. Both work together both go hand in hand. It is white and black, blue and white it is the Ying and Yang. Definitely without a shadow of a doubt the Ying and Yang and this humanity do not know because all seek to dominate control and destroy. We refuse to learn and know that the more we destroy is the more we kill and destroy ourselves.

There is a natural balance well was a natural balance but right now God chaos looms because no one truly knows that the earth shifts and is aligning with chaos and this chaos will come to man soon and very soon.

Lovey all this humanity need to know because each one can save themselves but they have to come to you truthfully.

God they know their time is near because they have a mandate before 2032 if there is no significant changes in the world humanity will not see 2132 because they have the three (3) dates which are 1313, 2032, and 2132 were given these three dates.

Lovey I know 2032 is significant but what will happen to humanity I don't know. Maybe the oil sands like I said will dry up but I know if we do not do something significant to save the environment then humanity can kiss their lives goodbye. God I know many are saying we are going to die anyways but I say to all this is negative thought because God never gave us death he gave us life and in all that we do in our lives we live for death and not for life.

Many of us do not know what constitutes death of life not the death of flesh. May of us still refuse to accept that the flesh is a prison for the spirit because in all that we do and the pleasures that we seek in enjoyed by the spirit and not the flesh because the spirit is life and no one in humanity can kill the spirit apart from you yourself. This is the choice we make hence I will forever say we live for death and not life because none of us know what life truly is.

MICHELLE

God I have forgotten the exact distance to you because numbers play a key role in life. It is a part of life a signature to you. Seven numbers have you and man the distance is so far my waves – wavelengths to you take so much time because it have to travel a distance in time and each day killing grows the further you get from me and humanity.

Everyone Lovey has the key to change but everyone refuse to trust live for truth – life

Lovey when will humanity learn? I just hope before it's too late.

God what purpose does it serve a man to kill – deceive when he knows his pay her pay is death.
Death of mind body and soul – spirit
Death of all
This planet

Lovey no man owns this earth or anything upon this earth because at the end of his time lifetime he dies and leaves it all including his or her home in the grave.

This earth is not permanent God because a man cannot own that which he never had.
No man or beast was given this earth not even woman so don't get it twisted. Earth is a vacation home yes one of the party central, humanity – man just became trapped in it and refuses to leave it. But with all that they do they have to leave, leave it behind because man was allotted a time and after that time the flesh dies but the spirit lives on.

No one can take a piece of earth with them because earth too hath life because it is able to sustain and maintain them for only a short time

Lovey there is a vast universe out there that is full of live – beauty but man – humanity cannot see this because all they see and can see is the flesh

They fail to realize that the flesh is just a trap a prison for the spirit/soul. Lovey no one can measure the soul because no one can measure life nor can they measure death.

Lovey tell me can a man measure his sins so how can a man measure his spirit/soul?

Lovey it is beyond me how man and humanity claim to know but yet know nothing. Life and death cannot be measure because man cannot measure time. All that he thinks and know about time is naught because true time does not run on evils time and all of humanity is living on evils time hence the measure time in hours and have a 24 hour day. Lovey this isn't true time because nothing is done in truth. No man and yes no evil can measure time because time cannot be measure and no one can measure the truth.

God can a man measure you come on now. We don't even know you.

Tell me something Lovey can a man see his back without the aid of a mirror or someone? So if he cannot see behind him how can he see infront of him? No come on Lovey for real. If we cannot see behind us how can we see infront of us?

No Lovey in all that we do and claim to do do we truly know? We base everything on the science of humanity but yet fail to see the big picture that the science of humanity means nothing because within our genes lies the key to life and death and no man hath the key to life and death except for you. I know revelations of their bible say the angel have the key to death but he does not have the key to life so therefore this angel cannot be true because if he had the key to death he would have the key to life so therefore this angel cannot be from you or of you. You have to have both because life and death is the key to life human life and spiritual life but not good life because good life cannot die only evil or bad life dies and this humanity need to know.

Lovey as humans we say we cannot see you and we can't because none can see you around them – us so how can we say we know you and know where we are going if our eyes cannot behold you magnificent beauty and honey you are gorgeous. No come on Lovey you are infinitely gorgeous and magnificent who wouldn't want to hold your hand all day long come on now. Do you know how soft and caressing your hands are? No Lovey do you know the gentleness of your hands. I do trust me I do and yes that's why I yearn to hold them feel their tender touch. You have great hands. No no no definitely no do not change them keep them like this just for me.

Sorry people but hey I can't help it I am just weird like that now back on track.

Lovey man knows not life or time so we – humanity cannot possibly know you.

MICHELLE

Go we have failed

Tell me something God why does spiritual evil put a pit before me each and every time I am on my way to success?

God no come on now. I've talked a lot about physical wickedness and all that is to happen to humanity if we do not change our ways but as for me spiritual wickedness refuse to leave my door – refuse to leave me alone.

They keep setting these pits for me to fall in and frankly God I am fed up of it hence I say we have failed.

God spiritual wickedness is no joke it is real and that powerful. God no one has ever conquered spiritual wickedness because no one dares talk about it and its origins.

No one knows how spiritual wickedness use the dead to carry out its evil deeds. No one has seen the councils of the dead and lived to tell about it but I am not running I am telling because the truth needs to be known. Humanity can accept the truth or reject each one of us have and has a choice. This is will the right to chose either good or bad. We cannot pick both we have to pick one – life or death and I am choosing life which is you.

Lovey and God the council of the dead are men and they talk amongst each other – bicker because the truth must not be known. The daughter of the dead – sin has been born but is she truly blue that powerful?

God for those that do not comprehend or overstand the council of the dead in the spiritual realm are all men but with the confines of the planet earth they are both male and female and of different nationalities. They are like unto the United Nations with the different nations the only exception for this united nation is that they sit as one council and are the head of the Roman Catholic Church. This organization and council is the spearhead for evil because Satan governs this church personally as well as oversees its day to day happenings meaning spearheads of war. Strife it generates with other nations.

God Allelujah I know differently because I have seen the truth and sacrifices must be given. I know what BIC stands for because she is one of the daughters of six the second 6 in the formation of hells unholy union but in truth she is the first in this day and time. She is the first daughter of Satan and there is two more to go. God Allelujah the devil once again have another spawn and once again true evil has been born but all must come to an end because in truth we are all the devils own in some way or another because of sin. Lovey I am sorry because I am off course again I strayed.

Now back on board. God this spiritual evil – this dead man that died he set his pots four (4) pots of oats cooking – boiling. I did not see a stove or hot plate but the pots of oats of this dead man was boiling. God there is more because it started with me walking to a tennis court to play tennis and we had to wait for the court and when one became empty someone else took it and I said we have to wait our turn meaning the next person get the court that is waiting in line so he relinquished the court but it, not the first time this particular court is being used in my visions and food is being used but it's the first time the dead and this huge hole was infront of me. God the hole was dug and you can see the mountain of dirt meaning the dirt was piled high leaving a sink hole. There was hardly any room to play and I kept hitting the ball in the hole. I could not hit the ball over the hole and my son kept hitting the ball every which way.

Lovey I will not finish this one I am going to leave this unfinished not because of spiritual evil or physical evil but here is not the right place and time for this so I will leave it alone. The less said the better at times because Lovey I know you will not fail me it is I to fail you and trust me I am not trying to fail you.

Lovey and God no matter the course of action evil takes I know for a fact that evil is born and no one can change this. I know evil gets in through the back door and I know the back door is our genes. Evil is within all of us because this is our makeup and no human being on the face of this planet can dispute this. We all have the genes of sin within us including me. It is a part of our spirit heredity. Hence today God I am coming to you again and I am asking you to take the sinful gene from my gene pool. Lovey I do not want or need the genes of sin within me I did not choose this my forefather's chose it and I relinquish the genes of sin and accept all that is good and clean.

Lovey because I did not know this and I am just finding this out I am choosing for my children all that is good and I am asking you to take the genes of sin from their gene pool. Lovey as I come to you with sincerity truth honest and true love please take all that is evil and sinful from their genetic gene pool and Lovey whatever you do in the name of goodness and truth please infinitely please take the sinful gene all of it from my genetic off springs. God if life is extended please infinitely never ever let anyone that is from my bloodline that is born to my children and grand children and so on for infinity and beyond be born with the sinful gene (s). God Lovey everyone must only have the good gene which is the gene (s) of life, truth, honesty, goodness and Lovey they must have all your goodness and truth so they can see you and communicate with you face to face in a clean and righteous place.

Lovey I am just figuring this out that the gene of sin is within us. This is the truth of sin because this is how sin is truly born.

God humanity does not know this. I did not know this until today May 31, 2012. Lovey this is I don't even know what to say because I am at a loss. This is why we get old and nothing else because sin is a part of our DNA.

God I knew sin was old and wrinkly but for us to be born with it and now I know the truth of the saying we are born in sin and shaped in iniquity.

Lovey how do I truly save me and my family because now I truly do not know.
Lovey how can we truly be clean if we have the gene of uncleanness within us?

Lovey as for my peeps true loved ones and friends I want to chose for them and my mind is aching to do so but I cannot. I cannot chose for them because I would be taking away their right which is the right you gave for them but if anyone say chose why did you not chose for me then God I ask you with pure love and truth that you take the gene of sin from them and their children and their children's children for infinite lifetimes.

Lovey I need all that is right and good from you. Lovey many things I truly don't know and as I move on in life things are being revealed to me.

God I am still amazed at finding this out. I know this my mother and grandmother did not know and if it be thy will please I am asking you to forgive them because I know they did not know this because if they did they would not have chosen the sinful gene to be in their children.

Lovey and God humanity now knows this let's now hope they make the right decision for themselves as well as their children and offspring.

Lovey thank you for revealing to me the truth because now we truly know that the GENES IS hence the beginning – Genesis.

MICHELLE

God what is this great force in the darkness that cannot be seen but yet hath great power?

It has power to speak to you
Power to control your spirit
Power to make your spirit stand still

God it is not an evil force but the power of its pull is great extremely powerful so powerful that you cannot get out of its grip.

God is this negative energy?
I've classed this energy as being evil because I do not know where this force comes from.

More time it's a man behind this energy but this energy you cannot see the person behind it so I come to you now and ask you about this great force that holds the spirit at bay.

God this force in the darkness is real but its not an often occurrence meaning it's not all the time this force comes to me. It's seldom to rare but this force is there. At times you feel as if you are going to die because the pulling action is like a great magnet pulling you towards it hence I have called this energy force as evil but if it's not please forgive me because I lack comprehension of this force.

God please give me wisdom and sight to overstand and comprehend this force. It is the pulling action that I do not comprehend so can you please help to explain it because I am at a loss as to how and why this happens.

Yes there is great force in the darkness but yet with this darkness you cannot see the person within this darkness but you can speak to him. You know the person is there but the darkness overshadows him therefore you cannot see him. Hence I say there is life in the darkness meaning light in the darkness that neither the spiritual eye nor the physical eye can see.

God is this power good because I do not know. I have to come to you and question you because I know this power and person is not you.

God what is this gate that this person is able to go to. It's like a steal door out of ancient days gone by. God who is this man in the darkness and why does he have so much power and pull to overpower the spirit at will.

MICHELLE

God as my body overheats thank you for sending the breeze to cool me down because you know just how hot my back can get and how miserable I can be.

I love the heat to a large extent – degree because I sweat and burn off a couple calories and this I love to do. I can lose a couple pounds hopefully. Yes it's hard by I have to try and yes I know I need to be a lot more active.

I need to tone up my body and hopefully this summer I can do that as well as continue to sport my new look which is heavenly and infinitely divine.

God I needed this new look and trust me if I can have my way I am going to keep this look forever ever. No God come on my head is freeeeeeeeeeeeeeeeeeeeeeeeeeeeeeeeee truly free too bad you can't let me sport the complete silver look. Yes the whiter than paper look. Lovey I am happy with my hair. Yes it's the nappy as pappy look but who cares I am so inlove with it. Lovey you know this is me the shorter than short hair. No I cannot go bald but if I could trust me I would but truly I am fine the way my hair is now. Hey no more Don King look.

Lovey I am just happy with my hair that's all because my hair suits me just fine and yes perfectly.

Lovey I truly hope you are happy with my hair because I did lighten my burdens – my heavy load. I know you are not disappointed because I am happy and I know you would rather me be happy than sad. Also I hope we can carry on in peace and love true love and harmony. And Lovey no complaints when it comes to my hair because I know you and don't even go there because I know the daughters of heaven have short nappy hair because I saw them.

Love you lots so you can't complain.

True love always you are my dear.

MICHELLE

God when freedom comes let the world be free – happy

God when freedom comes for me let me truly find you in good cheer

Let my life be blessed with you and happiness
Let my life and your life be filled with good prosperity
Let us fly in your goodness
Be truly free

God when freedom comes let it fin us truly together and happy
Let it find us in each other's arms
Let laughter float
Light up the earth
Let true freedom reign forever

God when freedom comes
Rescue the earth from all unclean beast and spirit
Let her find herself again
Rebuild her anew

God when freedom comes
Rescue the earth from all unclean human beings and let earth bask in the goodness of your truth, your harmony and your true love

God when freedom comes let earth be brand new but this time around for me and your people let no evil in nor let anyone destroy her goodness and let us all live in true peace the true goodness of you God for all eternity.

MICHELLE

God the damage has been done man have polluted everything and the devil has another spawn that was born upon the face of the earth

God we now have radioactive water
Radioactive food – fishes

God man knows not what he has done because humanity and all that is on earth will be his stomping ground – his evil domain

Now the pollution of other lands have reached others now toxic waste will be unleashed upon the countries of other lands

God this will wreak havoc on man because the dragon have done its now woe be unto man because all have become contaminated – impure not good to eat.

God in all that man do and does we seek to destroy and we do destroy

The filth of other nations will always contaminate the land because man fail to realize that one sin affect nations, other lands – the entire earth

God humanity cannot see that one sin pollutes us all
Pollutes the entire globe
Affect all humans – humanity

God what can be done to save man because you have tried and failed meaning you give them the truth and instead of walking in the truth and living by the truth humanity lives in lies and live to die.

God humanity does not want saving because if humanity did there would not be so much killing, hatred, bloodshed, uncleanness upon the land.

God I know the wails of man but I cannot cry all I can say is woe be unto man because we would not listen and heed the true warning signs that you have given.

MICHELLE

God it matters not if we kill each other by warfare anymore because man – humanity is destined to die

The waterways have become polluted
Humanities garbage now drifts – floats

Waterways unclean and the beast have done nothing to clean it amend its dirty ways and now the first woe is upon the earth and man will continue to ignore it. Soon they will find no good food to eat and then they will cry cry to you God but I know you will ignore their cries because long ago they did not listen and today they are still not listening.

No God none will remember their sins because their sins are forgiven atoned for by one man. A man that does not exist - a man that never lived.

Man will suffer and like Bob Marley said many more will have to suffer and many more will have to die. This is so true infinitely true man will die. The dead carcass will be many cemeteries will overflow hell will have plenty of room.

New diseases will now plague humans all brought to life because the Beast polluted the waters – seas and soon man will not be able to swim amongst the fishes of the seas because the beast made it so. He polluted the waters with its radioactive crap – chemicals.

Who will hold the Beast accountable God certainly not man because humanity goes along with what the Beast and its allies have done.

Who will hold the Beast accountable God for destroying all that you have created all that we had? Now the fishes are no longer safe. They now travel to other lands polluting our waterways – our good meat food that we eat.

Woe yes this is the first woe of many to come because for a surety starvation will now be upon the land?

MICHELLE

Woe Woe Woe
God Woe

Dear God hear my woes because death cometh in a new form

The seas are no longer safe
The waters have been touched
Man did not heed your warning signs now revelations have been unleashed

The beast is here God that great snake of old but this time he's fatter and he devours at will

Woe be unto the earth because we've polluted all that we eat and now we will become food and preys' for the Snake and his allies

The disease of the flesh is here
Woe be unto Canada – all the lands
Woe be unto the fishes of the sea because man will no longer be able to consume
Woe God woe be unto man

The drinking waters God the drinking waters
Woe be unto man because they too will become contaminated

Woe be unto man God
Woe be unto man because the flesh eating disease is here and it rears its ugly head

Man kills
Humanity dies
The beasts – animals in the fields die
Life in the waters will now perish and the beast would have won. He would have done his job by destroying humanity and every living thing in his sight.

The snake would have won God
The great serpent of old would have won because man refused to listen now doom and gloom walks the earth

God woe be unto man because the serpent is here and all his people have and has gathered to see his child. This is their savour but woe be unto them. Woe be unto man.

Woe be unto man God woe be unto man because they did not heed your warning signs they listened to unclean men that lead their souls all the way to hell but God not all is lost because I know you will step up and send humanity your people a savour to save them.

I know you will show your strength and rise her up – the one to save humanity. She's the one to rise up the one to defeat the snake and the dragon and all their allies.

God when the clean and righteous one comes to not let your people be deceived because the snake is not only wise but he is cunning. He has gained access to time travel because he jumps in and out of time zones at will. He has had many centuries to learn of the back door and trust me he uses it at will but his fire can be extinguished on earth God but in hell he shall surely burn. Man know not of this fire but then I did tell them of the spiritual fire and containment unit that will house sin – Satan.

God woe be unto man God
Woe be unto man because every nation will now feel the destruction and devastation of the dragon and woe be unto man because they did pollute the waters and the land and no one can stop the dragon because his is already done.

Woe be unto man God woe be unto man because Satan did sire his daughter now woe be unto man because the deed has been done and earth will be his stomping ground soon and very soon.

Woe God woe be unto man because the dragon did sing it spued its damnation unto man but man still cannot see. They cannot see their own destruction – downfall and death upon this planet the home we call earth – Mother Earth.

MICHELLE

Woe mi belly God
Woe the end of man – humanity draws near

Woe mi belly God Woe devastation have reached the land
Man is doomed
The devil's society has won
They carry everyone to hell with them now man will face the judgment of sin because God you judgeth no one.

Humanity did not listen
They did not heed your calling
Did not heed your cries now death will take more because the dragon did its job polluted the seas with Cadmium – deadly radiation.

God woe mi belly it will not be fun for humans – humanity

God woe mi belly humanity made fun of you disrespected you and now the dragon has won because no one was looking their eyes were on the wrong prize.

Starvation starvation now man will truly know how it feels to dance with the devil – evil. They refused to learn now every nation will have to bow down to this beast – the serpent – snake. But in fact this snake is not new he's the same beast of old but this time around he's a little wiser smarter and fatter because he got access to time – extended time.

He learnt the points of entry to time therefore he has his allies and they will devour man

We were the ones meaning humans were the ones to give him access to the portal of time. Many have forgotten the increasing portal yes the ozone depletion.

Now the beast is fully in. Yes he's fat and powerful because we the humans made him grow. We gave him new life now he's fatter and stronger than before.

We gave him the blood of saints many sold their souls to him and now his new world order will unfold – take shape and woe be unto man because he will enslave yet again and cause all humanity to truly bow down to him. He will kill at will and no one will be saved or be saved and safe because we all gave evil access to our souls and we will be his domain. We will be controlled by him because we made it so – this way. Woe be unto those that sold their souls. Woe be unto them because they too will die because the devil and evil favours no one not even his own.

MICHELLE

THE GREATER THE LIE THE DARKER THE MASK

God it is not if this is so it is so – the greater the lie the darker the mask. This has nothing to do with colour of skin this has to do with sin – the lies of sin because all evil tells you is a lie – wrong.

When we commit sin do we not lie to cover it up?

Do we not run and hide in hopes that we will not get caught?

Tell me something can a man truly run from the truth?

Can the truth lie?

Can the truth die?

Now tell me why do we believe in lies? Why do we not know the truth?

Any man that telleth a person – humanity that they have to die to achieve life tell him or her that I say they are a liar because they do not know God nor do they represent God. No one I repeat no one have to die to see God or be with God. Remember you were told and never forget it **THE WAGES OF SIN IS DEATH BUT TRUTH IS LIFE EVERLASTING.** So if you know this why are you listening to people that you you have to die in order to see God or go to heaven.

Tell me something when did God tell any of you that he was the death angel?

When did God tell any of you that you have to die to see him?

Our problem is as humans we believe and none of us know.

Absolutely no one can believe in God you have to know God. Any one that tells me I have to believe in God I will tell them to get thee behind me and kiss my ass because belief is not faithful to God. Infinitely trust me on this belief is a sin a grave sin and this is why I tell each and every one of you to **_KNOW_** God and not believe. The reason for this is anyone can come to you and say try my religion because our religion is right. We pray to God, read the bible, have bible practice and prayer meetings, you can be elected to different positions in our church, you can be ordained to be a minister or pastor, you can go to theology school if you want to but it is not a prerequisite, you can get married, have children, our way is true because we praise God and do all that God tells us to do as outlined in the bible. We teach you about Jesus because Jesus is the way and the light and you have to be born again in order to see God this is why God gave us his only begotten son. He shed his blood for us so that we will be saved. If you don't believe in Jesus you cannot see God nor can you enter into his kingdom. Jesus is the way and there is no other way because the bible said so and the bible is the truth of God it is divinely inspired by God.

Ah yes God I have heard this story over and over again and this is why I get down on my people who are our family and say if you believe in this crap continue believing because none of them know you God.

Lovey who the hell does the church think they are fooling with crap like that and this is why I keep telling you God and will forever drill it in your head that the full truth must be known. You cannot allow humanity to believe in lies and if you continue to let them believe in lies then humanity can hold you guilty of sin because you lied to them meaning you kept the truth from them and caused them to sin. I keep telling you God that you cannot let humanity hold you guilty of sin because of the crap and filth that we do. Give them the full truth and if they continue to follow sin then you cannot be guilty because you gave them the full truth without a shadow of a doubt.

God you know evil has stolen your identity because evil is a liar and a thief. Evil caused humanity to turn their backs on you as well as disrespect you so you cannot be like evil you have to separate yourself from evil by living by the truth.

Humanity have truth in them but we chose lies because evil is in our genes. I just discovered this yesterday. This is how evil gets in because we did marry evil and have children with evil. It is up to us now to choose right by asking you to take the genes of sin from our body mind and soul meaning our spirit. We are to ask you for this for our children as well because none of us can come to you dirty. We as humans have to know what is clean from what's dirty. We also have to know what is automatic death meaning what sins are forgiven and what sins are not and when I say forgiven I mean what sins are atoneable for meaning you can make atonement for otherwise what sins we can make repentance for.

God the devil has us lying and living in lies for him. He has us believing in the Mother and Child bullshit and none of us know that the Mother and Child analogy is Mother and Daughter. This the Roman Catholic Church uphold until this day and they refuse to tell humanity the truth. The mother represents spiritual and physical evil because she is the one to give birth to the three daughters of sin. When evil dies meaning an evil person in the physical realm dies before they die they have to pay homage to sin meaning tell sin that they love her. If they don't do it at death they have to do it in the grave. They have to stay true to sin meaning they love sin have to love her and this is why I tell people anyone can say they love you but it's not everyone can say they truly love.

God love belongs to the devil – evil but true love belongs to you God. When you have true love you do not desire the evils of this world nor do you want or need to be associated with sin or evil you want to be separated from them and if anyone was to read Psalms One (1) of their book of lies no it should be their book of death which is the bible they will see the prescribed way of life how to live.

Good cannot associate with evil because evil pulls and make you one of them sinful. God one cannot be good and the other evil because evil over powers good and cause good to become unclean. So if you are good and that person is unclean there is no way that you can become clean. You have to separate from that person.

Good must separate from evil in all that he or she does.

Good cannot eat mean of unclean beasts this will cause you to become unclean

Good cannot sit in the council of the wicked this will cause you to become unclean

Good cannot eat with the wicked and unclean this will cause you to become wicked and unclean

Good cannot marry unclean mean or women this will cause you to become unclean and this too will cause your children to become unclean

Good must not commit adultery like sinners do because this will cause God to turn from you and even despise you. This too causes you to be unclean and it is an abomination unto God because God hath children but he does not have more than one mate

Good must follow and adhere to the laws of God not the laws of man because God is not governed by the laws of man he is governed by his laws and one of those laws is thou shalt not kill. With God it is not death for death but life for life and we must live for life which is the truth.

Evil cannot say they were with God because no evil has ever resided with God or lived in his kingdom – abode because God is not unclean he is clean

Evil cannot say you can live forever because it is not all of us that live forever. Know that evil sin and death must die but truth which is life lives on forever

A dirty man or woman cannot say they know God and continue to do wrong they knoweth not God but knoweth the ways of sin and death

A dirty man or woman cannot say they know God and commit adultery they knoweth not God but knoweth the ways of sin and death

A dirty man or woman cannot say their child is of God and commit sin their child is not of God but of sin because that child knoweth sin because sin is embedded in their genes – DNA

No woman or man can stay they are pure and clean not even I can say this all I can say is show me your ways and I will show you your sins and my sins.

Knowing God is to know sin but it does not mean you are to walk in sin nor does it mean you are to live in sin

Life is given truthfully to man – humanity but death is given in sins and lies

Life is true to truth but death can only be true to lies

Death cannot take a life that is not given to him it can only take lives that are given hence death is true to death but cannot be true to life

Know the difference between life and death

Know the spiritual and physical realm because life and death is not the same in the spiritual hence we say man – humanity dies but in truth the flesh decays – dies in the physical but the spirit and soul lives on.

Death hath no command over the spirit nor does he have any command over life so death like I said cannot take a life unless it is given because in truth the spirit moves on for sentencing while the flesh of the body rots – decays. Hence I will drill it in your head and tell you the life you live on earth determines where you go in the spiritual. No man can dispute this not even God because it is so. Good and evil knows this and God cannot change this to suit anyone not even me.

God gave each and every one of us Will meaning the right to chose good or evil which is also known as life and death it is up to each one of us to make a choice. I cannot choose for you because if I did I would be wrong and I would be taking away your right. Yes I can choose for my children because they are a part of me and because I know the truth now I have told God of my desires of truth and goodness for my children and my family. It is not to say that my children cannot relinquish this they can by asking God not to be a part of their lives when they get older but I am hoping that they will stay with God because God is right and truthful.

And no God cannot sin you or charge you with sin for choosing that which is right and true for your children. You know the goodness of God always choose good for them. Even before you have children ask God for good children and please please please ask God to take the genes of sin away from your children. This is vital because this is the genes that cause us to sin and lie hence we become old and die. Never forget these sayings:

THE WAGES OF SIN IS DEATH BUT TRUTH IS LIFE EVERLASTING
AND
THE GREATER THE SIN THE DARKER THE MASK

The greater the sin the darker the mask is something I got this morning and trust me my spirit will not let me forget it. I was lazy because I did not get up to write it down. Listen people there are times when I am lazy I don't want to get up to write something down and I didn't but my spirit did not let me forget the quote hence you have it in this book.

I know there is a greater and more significant meaning behind this quote and as I read it I know this quote is extremely important and true.

As humans we are living in darkness and many are saying you are a liar because I have Jesus well I am telling you no one can save you of your sins except you yourself. You have to protect your soul and clean yourself up no one can do that for you. And no you cannot pay someone to clean your soul because no one know you better than you yourself.

God gave you a spirit it is yours to keep. You can't give it to someone else to take care of you have to take care of it. Yes some people have sold their souls they made that choice to sell it and like I said there is no givesy backsy. If you sell your soul to the devil you cannot say in the grave I am going to live with God because Jesus is going to save me even before this you cannot say on your death bed God take my soul and save me of my sins. Trust me the devil will laugh at you and God will shake his head and turn his back on you. God will not save you because you forgot you made a contract with the devil and that contract is binding it cannot be nulled or voided it is for life and that life extends to the spiritual world. Remember the life you live in the physical determines where you go in the spiritual. Well if you gave the devil your life in the living it is binding in hell and death. The devil's contract cannot be broken so don't expect God to step in and save you. You were the one to nullify and void your life. You gave it away. You told God that you didn't want him. You told God to leave you alone because the offerings of the devil suits you just fine. God will not help you nor will he void the contract you have with Satan and death. If God did then he would be a liar and yes he God would have to let all of humanity into his kingdom because he broke the law. His own law and like I said God cannot break his own law (s) to please me or anyone. Right is right and God must live right he cannot live wrong.

And anyone that say they can blame God for death you cannot. Go back to the beginning of your book of death – ¼ truth which is your bible. Read it again meaning the part when God said to Eve the day you eat of the fruit you shall surely die. God told her the truth and she ignored God and walked on the way of sin hence she died. She had children for sin hence sin became a part of our genes – DNA.

You can relinquish this gene by asking God not to let your children be born with it if you are going to have children. God cannot refuse you this and this you must teach your children. And yes people for those who are going back to Noah this is how sin got back in on earth after the great flood. Sin did not escape to another planet sin was always here on earth because sin is in our genes.

So Noah and his children including his wife had the genes of sin in them?

Yes and so do I including you hence you know that sin can never possess anyone sin is born and no I am not going to get into possession because no one can be possessed by demons because demons hath not the authority to possess any one because evil is in all of us. We can give ourselves totally over to sin and when we do so we have to live and act according to sin. We know this from the cross because the cross is a part of sin the only exception today is we turn the cross upwards and not downwards. And no people the cross is not the mark of the beast it is infinitely 666 but the devil has a line atop the 666 whereas his daughters have the 6 lying down. Each one have a 6 laying down hence the trinity and yes the mark of the beast 666. So when you use the mark 666 you are not representing Satan himself you are representing his daughters. To represent Satan you have to put a straight line above and below the 666 and that is just for Satan but the female Goat that you have with the five pointed star does not represent Satan it represents true evil meaning the woman that evil must go back to. She is the one receive the life of evil not Satan the man but Satan the woman – female goat as you depict her. And no Satan is not as powerful as her she is the giver of evil life and she is the taker meaning at the end of evil's life cycle on earth they meaning wicked and evil people is received by her.

For those who remember I think it is Nicodemus in your bible where he asked when a child is born can they go back into his mother's womb and Jesus said not unless he is born again. Now you know the meaning of that parable. And the answer is yes because like I told you above wicked and evil people and sprits must return to their mother at death and this is why the church preach and tell you that you have to be born again. They tell you you must be born again or you will not see God but they don't tell you that the person you see is the God of sin.

Good cannot be born again because good continues on to greater life and knowledge. Evil dies at death because evil lives to kill and destroy.

Good life cannot be destroyed because it knoweth not sin meaning it is good and cannot sin and please don't look to humanity and say a baby hath not sin because I told you we are born with the genes of sin. Our parents did not commission God before we were born for good clean and truthful children. Children that will follow in his God's true and righteous footsteps. You know this now so ask God for forgiveness. God cannot punish you for what you do not know know this. Many things I did not know in my past but now that I know I have to teach my children and teach you. Yes we are held guilty but if you do not know something you just don't know as for the people in the grave it's a different story because many did not know. Some will go directly to hell but it all depends on your good deeds. Your good must outweigh your bad. I cannot change this nor can God change this. Right is right and there is no exception for me or you or them. All you can do is pray for them and petition God truthfully to help them like I have done for my mother grandmother and family. I don't know if my goodness will count for anything or if I have any goodness on my plate meaning records. If I do have and my goodness outweighs my sins then I have asked God to save my family and children which are my mother, children peeps true loved ones and friends. I refuse to let my goodness go towards saving wicked and evil people meaning people that knowing kill at will and hurt other human beings. No I God was to say Michelle have compassion on them I would tell God no I still refuse because I know my hurt at the hands of sin – wicked and evil people. I know the hurt they have caused God and the lies they have told on God so no I would not save them no matter how they cried or used their babies or say please save my baby I would not do it because none are truthful and faithful unto him God. No we cannot do evil and expect to get right come on now. God does hurt people just as how you feel pain and hurt God feels it too. Why should God shed anymore tears for us. We don't shed a tear for God. We don't care if we hurt him but yet when we do wrongs we want him to save us and have mercy upon us why should he?

We spit in his face each and every day.
We alter self
We live to die so why should God continue to maintain and sustain our lives
We know right from wrong but yet we teach wrong tell our children to do wrong and when the devil has us in its grip we say God forgive me I am sorry for what I have done. You know that what you did was wrong there is no forgiveness for that because you know your act or deed was wrong. Do not look to God for forgiveness for that wrong because no amount of good that you

do will allot you forgiveness for that sin from God. You willingly participated in the act. I too am guilty of this hence we are all guilty of sin.

Like I've said no one can look after you soul or spirit apart from you. You have control of it so secure it. This is your life and it's wrong for sin evil and death to take it unless it is given to them. God gave us all life he never gave us death we accepted death because of the lies sin told and that's why we did because we are living the life sin prescribed for us. God did not prescribe this life for us. We believe instead of knowing and none of us can blame God for the problems in our lives. I've told you there are spiritual wickedness and spiritual wickedness is strong. Spiritual wickedness are the ones to hinder good by putting pitfalls in your way as well as hinder your success. Evil will do whatever it takes to make a good person fail you have to know this and this is why many of us fail and yes die in the process because you became a threat to evil. Evil does not want to give up what he's got so he will eliminate every good people on the face of this planet to keep sin and death going. Sin knows he's going to die because like I've said death is true to death. This is his job and death too must die because it has taken the lives of the innocent because of sin.

And yes many people say they are good but end up being bad meaning do wrong they start off on the right path but end up on the wrong path for example, Solomon and many others that came after him.

When you are of God and following the pathway of God you cannot wine and dine with the devil you will become unclean and you will fall yes die this is why it is extremely important for good to separate from evil. Good cannot associate with the dead this is infinitely wrong and yes this is why evil torment us because we are living amongst the living dead meaning the begotten of the dead now you comprehend and overstand revelations when it talks about the first begotten of the dead and yes where it also said Jesus is the first begotten of the dead. We are all a part of the living dead every human being on the face of this planet the only time you no longer become a part of the living dead is when you are separated from the devil and his people. You are living right and doing right by God but you cannot do it living amongst evil because the next person's sins do affect you.

Remember as it is in heaven so it is on earth. In heaven good and evil is separated meaning heaven and hell is separated so why can't we separate ourselves on earth? Why does good have to cohabitate with evil and even marry evil? God isn't the one to be living and doing wrong humanity is because we don't do what God truly tells us to do. We know we are to separate from evil but yet we do not do it.

We know we are not to infinitely let evil including his race of people in our lands which are the Babylonians but yet we still do it and call it immigration and when they come in take your jobs and destroy your lands you cry and say it is the Christian thing to do. I guess you're right it is the devil's thing to do because Christians do not follow God nor do they worship God they follow and worship the devil because they commit every abominable act of sin in the sight of God then turn around and lie saying that they worship him. They even go so far as saying Jesus had a son when they know this is one of the greatest lie to ever be told on God. This lie goes so deep that it sickens my stomach then to add insult and salt to this great wound they take the lie even further and say God offered his son as a sacrifice to die on a cross for a sinful and whoring set of demons. You live for sin and the devil people and yes I use the B word but changed it. None of you live for God so how the hell can anyone of you say that you are going to live with God. None of you can tell me what God looks like. You all say you cannot see God but you can see God God is not dead. I say he's hiding but God hides from no one. When I say he's hiding I mean he is trillions of miles away from me hence the distance between the two is far and wide and this is due to sin and the sinful acts we commit on the face of the planet earth.

A part from the moon this is the only planet where bloodshed is predominant and even this analogy is incorrect because I have yet to see blood I've only seen the killings. This planet is where the war starts before it comes to earth hence man's fascination with the moon. This is the evil planet because it affects humanity in an evil way.

So in all that good do good must separate from evil and whether you like it or not this is the way it must be. God has kept this so from the beginning of time and it is still so because there is no evil or sin in his abode. We know we are to separate from sin but we look at what sin offers.

The money
The fame
The houses
The clothes
High end clothes and jewelry
The drugs
The sex with different partners
The desecration of body mind and soul
The eating of unclean meat
The worship of different gods
The control and dominion over other races
The hatred – prejudice
The lies
The killing and stealing

Everything that evil offers we accept including his lie that says one man came and died for you sin so that you will get into God's abode. All you have to do is accept him because he died for your sins and you have to accept his blood because he did shed his blood for you. All this you believe and like I said you do not know.

Tell me something did he not tell Eve she would not die and God told her she would die but she believed him over God and guess what she died with him. Now he's told you to accept Christ and blood and the entire world believes him and now is worshipping this man and guess what you are all going to go to hell with him. No you are going to go to heaven with him because his hell will be your heaven.

When does the lies stop people? The Babylonians are the ones that sacrifice lives onto sin you all know this just follow the history of their race. The human sacrifices within the Indian kingdom, the animal worship now tell me is this God? Is this what God wants for humanity? I've asked you before when did God become death?

Tell me when did God the true and living God become doctor death? Tell me and yes I am yelling at you people.

Look back from the beginning until now the present and tell me when did God the true and living God become a liar?

What lies has God My Love and Lovey ever told on any of you? So why are you believing in the lies of the devil and his people? Sin cares not for you so why do you care about sin? Sin steals your soul and say yes this is right when each and every one of us know that it is wrong.

<u>NO ONE CAN SAVE YOU EXCEPT YOU YOURSELF</u> so why are you being fooled by the devil and sin.

I've told you God does not lock anyone out of his kingdom we are the ones to lock ourselves out because we do not want to live clean and right.

Don't even bring up Satan and his people because God does not lock them out of his kingdom they can see God and live with God they are the ones to lock themselves out by spreading lies and hate. They are the ones to want control and dominion over the land and because they cannot have it they steal it, steal the Jew's identity meaning steal the identity of the true Jewish people this you call identity theft, they steal the identity of God but no one can steal God's identity because God is all but we will keep it this way for clarification purpose, they embed themselves in your land and country and when the time is right they enslave and destroy you and the time is coming when this will be done because you will have one government, one language, one currency, one religion because all religions will consolidate and all the languages will be consolidated because all spoken language cometh from one source.

1313
2032
2132

Three dates
Three times

Who knows what will happen because at the rate humanity is going no one will live beyond 2032. This is the date I see time and time again. Like I said I do not know what will truly happen it could be that the oil sands dries up, the glaciers recede to 25-15 percent and if this happens woe be unto man because rainfall will seriously diminish and starvation global starvation will be upon the land.

And if you think a great god is going to come from the sky to save you think again unless you are one of the ones to believe in UFO's. I am being sarcastic people. Hey you've watched too much sci-fi flicks.

There are no such things as aliens well no I should not say that because we are all aliens we travel from land to land. But when you look at other life in other galaxies and universe they are just like me and you with the exception of sight you cannot see them but they can see you even talk to you. This is what we call the spirit. Our spirit is pure energy just like there's but know this beyond the threshold of time evil cannot travel. It has no place in real time – true time but within the confines of the earth and moon evil does travel because these two spaces are the only places to let evil in.

Think of it as the sun and moon. As humans our body need both to survive and they work in unison but over time because of our destructive ways there is no longer a balance because we made it so. We have to destroy because of sin. We can change this and one way to do so is by separating from sin. We have to get rid of the genes of sin this is the only way man can survive what is to come.

We can no longer live for sin
We can no longer live to destroy

We have to live for life now

We have to live for the truth

We all want to live and maintain our future but we have to stop the killing and hatred and truly listen to the true and living God.

If God is saying Ron what you are doing is wrong listen and don't ever do that wrong again.

God will never tell anyone to commit or do wrong you know this therefore you have to stop doing your wrongs.

We say we are God's people well if God does not do wrong why are we doing wrong? We should be doing right all the time so none of us in our present state can say we are children of God because we do nothing for God nor are we like God because we seek to kill and destroy, control and dominate, live to hate, lie and cheat. All out we are sinners because we live in sin and not one of us on the face of this planet can say otherwise not even the little yiddy biddy baby that is born because not one of us asked God for a good truthful honest and clean child like him. Not one of us asked God for life a clean and wholesome, happy and joyful life.

Like I've said we live to die we do not live to live nor do we live for life – a good life.

Nope don't even come here and say you are wrong because I give to my church and I donate money to the poor, or I do this and this.

Baby love that don't make you good it just makes you sinful why because you do to get. You do not do out of true love nor do you do for God. All you do you do for sin.

Did you every say God I am truly doing this for you because I truly love you and I am passionate about all you do?

No you say then how can all you do be good. The donation do you not want a tax receipt or recognition for what you do.

Some of you if you adopt a child of a different nationality the whole entire world have to know about it.

Some of you adopt and I am going to go here black babies and you use them as handbags but when it comes to the basic needs of these black babies you cannot give it to them and yes I am talking about the hair. Some of these black and mixed babies hair look worse than a frigging raggedy Ann doll. Comb their damned hair. What the hell do you think you can have black babies and ignore their hair? Our hair is nappy, some like unto pepper grain comb your child's hair shit I am tired of seeing some of you celebs with black and or mixed babies and their hair is on kept. We black people can do it it's called a head tie. I know some of the kids don't want their hair combed they would rather the on kept look it just means they are nasty and I am speaking from experience.

Listen go to a black hair salon and get your child's hair done and don't put them nasty chemicals in their hair like perm. It affects the scalp over time.

There are detangling shampoos and conditioners that you can use any place that caters to the black hair products sell these and don't forget the hair food comb and brush.

Don't worry if you wash your child's hair and it shrinks it's natural. Our hair shrink when you wash it. Well true black people hair anyway because some people look black but guess what they are not black.

After you wash the hair if you can't cane row it then twist it if it can be twisted and do do plats if your child is staying inside but please comb your child's hair because if I see one more of you celebs not taking care of your black child's hair trust me I will get a hair blog and call your asses out.

I am going to be a bitch here and say this if you can't take care of a black baby don't have none because they are not accessories or hand bags for anyone they are humans not your damned token to find favour in the black or any community. Truly love them as your own and you will get true love in return.

I am sick of the nonsense with some of you and none of you white people get upset because you would not like it we blacks start adopting white babies and start parading them around like tokens for the world to see. And no don't use Michael Jackson in this because as sick as he was he truly loved his children this I know.

In what you do there must be truth honesty and true love. We all say we love but it's a very few that hath true love.

Don't even go there by saying I love my husband or I love my man or I love my wife my baby because all I got to say is the mistress down the street, the sugar daddy you have when hubby is not around. Baby if this is love I would hate to see what constitutes hatred in your book and like I said anyone can say they love but it's not everyone that can say they truly love. Know the difference between the two because true love does not hurt or cause anyone pain love does and that's why we love because love is not true it is pain. It hurts, it deceives.

Yes many can dispute this but guess what no one not even God can dispute the truth because the truth will forever stand in time. It stands the test of time because the truth is time, it is life and more importantly the truth is God and will forever be God in time.

I am going to stop here because this is supposed to be a little little talk so enjoy your day and please do not stress over sin. Just please take care of your soul because this belongs to you and no one has a right to take this from you. This is your life protect it because it is vital in the afterlife.

Like I've said before know the truth here don't wait until your are dead meaning you are in the grave to learn the truth because then it will be too late.

MICHELLE

Other books by Michelle Jean

Blackman Redemption

A Little Talk With God

More Talk

Saving America from a Woman's Perspective

Blackman Redemption – The Rise and Fall of Jamaica

My Collective – The Dark Side of Me

My Collective – The Other Side of Me

Ode to Mr. Dean Frasier